STUTTGART

BALLET

STUTTGART BALLET

Texte von/Text by
HORST KOEGLER

Fotos von/Photographs by
LESLIE E. SPATT

DANCE BOOKS LTD 9 Cecil Court London

First published 1978 by Dance Books Ltd.
9 Cecil Court, London WC2N 4EZ

Printed by BAS Printers Limited
Over Wallop, Stockbridge, Hampshire

ISBN 0 903 102 42 0

Book design by Peter L. Moldon

Half title / *Seite 1* :
Initials R.B.M.E. / *Initialen R.B.M.E.*
(Left to right / *Links—rechts*)
Marcia Haydée, Egon Madsen,
Richard Cragun, Birgit Keil

Title spread / *Titelseite*:
Poème de l'extase
Marcia Haydée, Egon Madsen

Stuttgart's Second Ballet Miracle

The real miracle is that the company is still alive! For all past experience would have led one to expect that the Stuttgart Ballet should die five years ago, together with its founder and beloved father figure, John Cranko. One has only to think what happened to the Ballets Russes when Diaghilev died in 1929, or to the Grand Ballet du Marquis de Cuevas after his death in 1961—and one really doesn't dare think what might happen to the New York City Ballet or the Ballet of the XXth Century should . . . .

Cranko hailed from the stable of Ninette de Valois, and thus represented that species of figurehead who think of the decades to come rather than becoming too entangled in issues of the day; but like his illustrious predecessors he never really bothered about what would happen to his company when he was no longer around. Cranko was much too obsessed with life and the present to care for the future: so much so that he had little patience or sympathy with those who asked him to define his longterm policy. So it is not just by chance that two of his ballets, two which perhaps showed him at his most vulnerable and personal, had titles suggesting the transitoriness of life: *Présence*, his ballet about Molly Bloom, Roi Ubu and Don Quixote, and *Brouillards*, his choreographic vignettes about various sorts of human encounters, most of which are open-ended, if they do not actually end with a question mark.

So great was the shock when, on 26th June 1973, Cranko died—not quite forty-six years old—absolutely appropriately for his way of life on a return flight after the company's third American tour. Who was to succeed him, he who had never squandered the least thought about building up a successor, thus proving that he had not learnt at all from Dame Ninette's lesson? Even worse: in his paternalistic way he had become the great father-figure of his company, much more than just the Artistic Director: a figure on whom everybody in the company was dependent; from the last of the corps de ballet to the administrative staff, they had all somehow become his children. Overnight the family had lost its father, and there was no preparation at all for such an event. Understandably, everybody was paralyzed.

Several years and two directorships later we can say

that what happened after Cranko's death was Stuttgart's second ballet miracle. Miracles, by their very nature, happen rather rarely: but that two miracles should happen within such a relatively short time is almost too good to be true!

Stuttgart's first ballet miracle happened in the sixties, when Cranko led the Stuttgart Ballet from provincial anonymity to worldwide renown. True, Nicholas Beriosoff had prepared the ground by instituting a firm working base with his productions of the classics, thus providing not only a constant standard of reference and challenge for the dancers; but also an unexpected draw for the public, who already during Beriosoff's time had formed the Noverre Society, both to further the case of the Stuttgart Ballet and to educate its audience to a better understanding and appreciation of the company's aims and achievements. Suddenly Stuttgart seemed to remember that it hadn't always sulked in ballet anonymity: not least during the—alas only six—years when Jean-Georges Noverre, just two hundred years earlier, had made Stuttgart one of the ballet capitals of Europe; and not during the even shorter spell of Paul Taglioni and his daughter Marie, when their ballet *Jocko, the Brazilian Ape* started from Stuttgart before going the rounds of the world.

But it was Cranko under whom the Stuttgart Ballet took off on its own international flights: he who lovingly nurtured and developed its *equipe* of principals, Marcia Haydée and Birgit Keil, Ray Barra, Richard Cragun, Egon Madsen and Heinz Clauss; he who, with the help of his ballet mistress Anne Woolliams, built up its fine *corps de ballet*; he who choreographed and produced the majority of the company's repertory, from the carefully rethought and dramatically strengthened classics through to his full-length creations such as *Onegin* and *The Taming of the Shrew*; he who lured Kenneth MacMillan to Stuttgart to let him mount the ballet which London refused to let him create and which as *Song of the Earth* turned out to be one of the ballet jewels of the sixties; he who recognized the affiliated school, making it one of the best in the country; and he who established the very close bond between the company and its ever-growing group of followers. Cranko put Stuttgart on the ballet map of the world and made Stuttgart a very ballet conscious city. This was the first Stuttgart ballet miracle, for nobody before would ever have thought Stuttgart was the type of city to fall in love with ballet.

The fact that under him the Stuttgart Ballet had grown such a strong feeling of family togetherness proved at the hour of his death the very best insurance policy that Cranko could have devised, for now the whole company felt personally responsible for the survival of his work. And thus it happened not that a single person was declared his artistic heir and director, but that an emergency committee was formed, consisting of Anne Woolliams, Marcia Haydée and Dieter Graefe (who had been Cranko's personal secretary and aide), to carry on. Now that they had become aware that there was not an individual personality to follow in Cranko's footsteps, the company itself shouldered the burden. It was the most democratic decision imaginable. The consequence was that not one single person left the company, although all of the soloists and most of the *corps* dancers were inundated with lucrative offers from other companies.

Thus the company banded even closer together; and this is what really kept it alive in a situation where everything seemed to point to its dissolution. And this has not basically changed in the years that have followed, though there have been, of course, some departures, the most lamented ones being the loss of the exquisite and elegant Judith Reyn and the transfer to Munich of the tempestuous and quicksilver Joyce Cuoco. Of all the German companies, Stuttgart during these years of trial has had the least turnover of dancers. It really is astonishing, and it shows that Cranko must have implanted something to which it is hard to put a name, but which must definitely be something more than just loyalty (which inevitably wears off over the years). Personally, I think it must have been something approaching love.

However, if the company had survived the severe trials of the period following Cranko's death, how much greater must have been their surprise when they discovered that just when the appointment of Glen Tetley as Cranko's successor seemed to signal a return to normality and the arrival of a new era in its young history, what had actually started was their second term of trial.

At the time, Tetley's appointment seemed, if somewhat daring, nonetheless only logical. Tetley was one of the world's most fecund choreographers, who, coming from a modern dance background, had recently assimilated more and more elements from the *danse d'école*; he had fruitfully collaborated with the company and Cranko had invited him to become its resident choreographer. One can easily imagine how perfectly they would have matched as choreographers: Cranko being the communicative dramatist and Tetley the pure and cool formalist.

Alas, without Cranko's presence, the atmosphere became rather too pure and cool, and too formalist, for the dancers and public alike, let alone the critics. And the almost total neglect of the classics, and Tetley's obvious disinterest in the maintenance of the Cranko repertory did little to strengthen one's faith in his directorial foresight, however much one might have admired his special choreographic gifts, different as they were from Cranko's all-round talent.

It is easy to see how frustrated the dancers, who had been brought up by Cranko and had been taught to identify with their roles, must have felt when confronted with Tetley's choreography, where they were expected to project nothing but act as ciphers in his magisterial mandarin prose. How much more so they must have felt when they watched an altogether different brand of dancers emerging at their side, consisting of some of Cranko's latest recruits or those who had been engaged by Tetley: swift, slim, efficient, technically speedily brilliant, with an almost athletic and clinically abstract approach to dance. What must have gone on in Haydée's head—she one of the world's greatest dramatic dancers—when she was finally forced to realise that drama was out and functional movement-mechanics were the order of the day? Nonetheless, it was obvious that the company were dancing better than ever before, and that there was a group of splendidly gifted youngsters who were improving all the time: Lucia Montagnon (formerly Isenring), Jean Allenby, Melinda Witham, Barry Ingham, Carl Morrow, Mark A. Neal, Christopher Boatwright, Christian Fallanga, to mention just the most spectacular candidates for future soloist status. What was less obvious was that the Cranko dancers, too, branched out considerably, acquiring an additional technical resilience and pliancy which helped them to add an altogether new dimension to their style, which took on a scintillating sheen and polish without losing anything of its original emotional depth and colour. One first spotted it in the very few performances of the classics that were given; one sensed it in the thrillingly danced performances of such repertory gems as Cranko's *Initials R.B.M.E.* and MacMillan's *Song of the Earth*; and one watched it blossom in the marvellous progress of Birgit Keil, who under Cranko had always seemed on the verge of becoming a dancer of the first rank but who had never managed to take the actual step. Under Tetley she finally left her first soloist status to acknowledge and confirm her rightful position as the company's leading classical ballerina, with Vladimir Klos as her legitimate *danseur noble* consort.

Despite all this, what easily might have happened was

that Haydée, Cragun, and Madsen could have left the company, dissatisfied with the Tetley régime, to start careers as freelance dancers (Clauss had been chosen to succeed Woolliams as director of the John Cranko Ballet School); while almost every company in Germany and many abroad would have loved to have Keil as prima ballerina (a position which Stuttgart refused her) with Klos as her partner. But it didn't happen! The Stuttgart Ballet passed its second—the Tetley—test with flying colours: the original Cranko equipe stayed on and mixed amicably and harmoniously with the Tetley newcomers. And when Tetley resigned at the end of the 1975/76 season, obviously having arrived at the conclusion that he was unlikely ever to be accepted either by the Stuttgart public or by the critics, there were at least some more differentiated attempts to judge his achievements more objectively. Those who were able to look at the state of things without prejudice had to admit that the company had never before looked and danced more spiritedly, and that Tetley had at least contributed some ballets which any company in the world would be proud to own, notably Voluntaries, Laborintus, Pierrot Lunaire and Le Sacre du Printemps.

That the Stuttgart Ballet survived these three difficult years after Cranko's death is what I consider Stuttgart's second ballet miracle. With Haydée taking over from Tetley as Artistic Director from the start of the 1976/77 season (a decision arrived at after much consultation between Hans-Peter Doll, the General Manager of the Wurttemberg State Theatre—of which the Stuttgart Ballet functions as one of three wings, the other two being the opera and drama companies—and the dancers) things seemed at last to be back to normal. That of course, does not mean that the Tetley years are completely forgotten, and that the company has tried to continue where Cranko had to leave. This couldn't happen, for Haydée is not a choreographer herself and so has constantly to look out for choreographers, agreeing not only to mount their existing works for the company, but also persuading them to create new works: a very difficult job when one realizes that almost all the top-rank choreographers of today are firmly associated with one or another company.

In her first season Haydée, who continues to dance and thus cannot be compared with such other women directors of worldwide renown, as Marie Rambert, Ninette de Valois, Lucia Chase or Beryl Grey, has happily been successful in luring MacMillan once again to Stuttgart where he choreographed with his intensely poignant Requiem to Faure's music, which many consider to be his very best ballet so far. And with Rosella Hightower's Sleeping Beauty production she has not only emphasised the long overdue return to a policy which considers the classics as the best basis for the type of company which the Stuttgart Ballet represents, but also generated a new audience enthusiasm, which in the last few years had become somewhat flaccid.

With the announcements of new ballets by John Neumeier and Jiri Kylián and the continued collaboration with MacMillan for the 1977/78 season, Haydée seems firmly decided to follow those guidelines set by Cranko, leading towards a genuinely creative future. Even better, in her first season Haydée, whose spellbinding power as a dance-actress has not in the least diminished, has been able to foster some quite remarkable young dancer talents such as Eileen Brady, Sylviane Bayard, Nora Kimball, Kurt Speker and Stephen Greenston, and in addition seen that some other dancers like Reid Anderson and Marcis Lesins have been given new, challenging parts, thus helping them further to cultivate their art. And in William Forsythe she has discovered among the corps dancers a budding choreographic talent who hopefully will develop in the wake of a Neumeier or Kylián, though without necessarily leaving the company.

Thus at the start of the 1977/78 season, the seventeenth after Cranko was appointed Artistic Director, and after its fifth American tour, the Stuttgart Ballet seems to have survived the severest ordeals and trials of its young history and just entered what all who wish the company well hope will become its second era of unbounded creativity.

The old Cranko spirit of togetherness flourishes as strongly as ever before, and there is the same strong projection of happiness which sets the Stuttgart Ballet apart from most of the other Western ballet companies (in this they seem rather like cousins of the Royal Danes). Long may they continue to spread their message of joy: our world of the late seventies is desperately in need of it!

Stuttgarts zweites Ballettwunder

Das eigentlich Überraschende ist, dass es die Kompanie überhaupt noch gibt! Allen Erfahrungen in der Vergangenheit zufolge, hätte das Stuttgarter Ballett rechtmässig vor fünf Jahren sterben müssen, zusammen mit seinem Gründer und seiner vielgeliebten Vaterfigur, John Cranko. Man braucht sich nur daran zu erinnern, was aus den Ballets Russes wurde, als Diaghilew 1929 starb, oder aus dem Grand Ballet du Marquis de Cuevas nach seinem 1961 erfolgten Tod—und man wagt kaum, daran zu denken, was einmal aus dem New York City Ballet werden wird, sollte eines Tages . . . oder aus dem Ballett des XX. Jahrhunderts, falls . . .

Wie alle diese Männer, so war auch Cranko, obgleich er aus dem Lager von Ninette de Valois stammte, die entschieden jene andere Spezies von Kompanieleitern repräsentiert, die in die kommenden Dezennien vorausschauen, statt sich zu sehr von den heute aktuellen Dingen gefangennehmen zu lassen, nie wirklich darum besorgt, was aus dem Stuttgarter Ballett werden würde, sollte er eines Tages nicht mehr da sein. Er war viel zu sehr mit dem Leben und der Gegenwart beschäftigt, um sich viel Gedanken um die Zukunft zu machen—so sehr in der Tat, daß er wenig Geduld und Sympathie für Leute hatte, die von ihm eine Erklärung über seine langfristige Politik erwarteten. So ist es denn auch nicht reiner Zufall, dass zwei seiner Ballette, die ihn uns vielleicht am verwundbarsten und persönlichsten zeigen, Titel hatten, die die Flüchtigkeit und Vergänglichkeit allen Geschehens andeuteten: Présence, *sein Ballett über Molly Bloom, Roi Ubu und Don Quixote, und* Brouillards, *seine choreographischen Vignetten über verschiedene Arten von menschlichen Begegnungen, die meist ein offenes Ende haben, wenn sie nicht gar mit einem Fragezeichen schließen.*

Umso größer war der Schock, als Cranko am 26. Juni 1973 starb, keine sechsundvierzig Jahre alt—wie es schien, absolut seiner Lebensart angemessen, auf dem Rückflug nach der dritten triumphalen Amerika-Tournee. Wer, um Himmels willen, sollte ihm nachfolgen—ihm, der nie einen Gedanken daran verschwendet hatte, einen Nachfolger aufzubauen, und der damit bewies, ein wie schlechter Schüler von Ninette de Valois er war. Schlimmer noch: auf seine paternalistische Weise war er zur grossen Vaterfigur geworden, entschieden mehr als bloßer Künstlerischer Direktor der Kompanie, von dem jedermann in der Kompanie mehr oder weniger abhängig war, der letzte Corps-de-ballet-Tänzer nicht anders als die Mitglieder seines Stabs—sie alle waren ja irgendwie seine Kinder geworden. Über Nacht hatte die Familie ihren Vater verloren, und auf diesen Fall war man überhaupt nicht vorbereitet. Verständlich, daß jeder wie gelähmt war.

Mehrere Jahre und zwei Direktorien später können wir sagen, daß, was nach Crankos Tod geschah, Stuttgarts zweites Ballettwunder darstellt. Wunder ereignen sich naturgemäss sehr selten. Daß sich jedoch gleich zwei Wunder innerhalb so kurzer Zeit ereignen, ist fast zu schön, um wahr zu sein!

Stuttgarts erstes Ballettwunder hatte sich während der sechziger Jahre ereignet, als Cranko das Stuttgarter Ballett aus provinzieller Anonymität zu weltweitem Ruhm geführt hatte. Es stimmt, daß Nicholas Beriozoff den Boden vorbereitet hatte, indem er durch seine Klassiker-Einstudierungen ein sicheres Fundament geschaffen hatte, und damit nicht nur den Tänzern einen ständigen Orientierungsstandard und eine permanente Herausforderung bot, sondern auch einen in diesem Ausmaß nie erwarteten Kassenmagneten für das Publikum installiert hatte, das sich schon zu Beriozoffs Zeit in der Noverre-Gesellschaft zusammenfand, die einmal die Arbeit des Stuttgarter Balletts fördern und zum anderen für ein besseres Verständnis seiner Leistungen und seiner Ziele sorgen sollte. Plötzlich schien sich Stuttgart daran zu erinnern, daß es nicht immer in der Ballett-Anonymität vor sich hingedämmert hatte. Zumindest nicht während der—leider nur sechs—Jahre, als Jean-Georges Noverre ziemlich genau vor zweihundert Jahren Stuttgart zu einer der Balletthauptstädte von Europa gemacht hatte—und auch nicht während der sogar noch kürzeren Ära Paul Taglionis und seiner Tochter Marie während der zwanziger Jahre des achtzehnten Jahrhunderts, als ihr Jocko, der brasilianische Affe von Stuttgart aus seinen Weg um die Welt antrat.

Doch es war Cranko gewesen, unter dem das Stuttgarter Ballett international Aufmerksamkeit auf sich zog—er, der liebevoll und sorgsam die Equipe seiner ersten Solisten nährte und aufzog, mit Marcia Haydée, Birgit Keil, Ray Barra, Richard Cragun, Egon Madsen und Heinz

Clauss an der Spitze—er, der mit Hilfe seiner Ballett-meisterin Anne Woolliams Stuttgarts prächtiges Corps de ballet aufbaute—er, der die Mehrzahl der Ballette des Repertoires choreographierte und inszenierte, von seinen intelligent neudurchdachten und dramaturgisch verstärk-ten Klassikern bis zu seinen abendfüllenden Kreationen wie Onegin und Der Widerspenstigen Zähmung, die zu seinem Firmenzeichen wurden—er, der Kenneth MacMillan nach Stuttgart lockte und ihm erlaubte, das Ballett zu machen, das London ihm verweigert hatte, und das sich dann als Lied von der Erde als eins der Ballettjuwelen der sechziger Jahre erwies—er, der die angegliederte Schule reorganisierte und zu einer der besten im Lande machte—er, der die enge Verbindung zwischen der Kompanie und ihrer ständig zunehmenden Publikums-gefolgschaft herstellte. Cranko etablierte Stuttgart auf der Ballettlandkarte der Welt und machte aus ihr eine sehr ballettbewusste Stadt. Das war Stuttgarts erstes Ballett-wunder, denn nie hätte bis dahin jemand geglaubt, daß Stuttgart der Typ von Stadt war, der sich in das Ballett hätte verlieben können!

Tatsächlich stellte sich dann in der fatalen Stunde seines Todes heraus, daß das unter ihm so auffallend gewachsene Gefühl der Familienzusammengehörigkeit die beste Versicherungspolitik war, die er sich hätte ausdenken können. Denn jetzt fühlte sich jeder persönlich verantwort-lich, daß sein Werk am Leben blieb. Und so geschah es, daß keine Einzelperson zu seinem künstlerischen Erben und Testamentsvollstrecker erklärt wurde, sondern ein Notko-mitee zusammentrat, bestehend aus Anne Woolliams, Marcia Haydée und Dieter Gräfe, der Crankos per-sönlicher Sekretär und Vertrauter gewesen war, um die Geschäfte weiterzuführen. Jetzt, da man sich darüber im klaren war, daß es keinen individuellen Nachfolger für Cranko geben würde, entschloß sich die Kompanie dazu, die Last seiner Nachfolge auf ihre kollektive Schulter zu nehmen. Es war die demokratischste Entscheidung, die man sich vorstellen konnte. Die Folge war, daß niemand die Kompanie verließ, obgleich jeder der Solisten und viele der Corps-de-ballet-Tänzer von anderen Kompanien mit lukrativen Angeboten überschwemmt wurden.

Auf diese Weise schloß sich die Kompanie noch enger zusammen. Und genau das war es, was sie in einer Situation am Leben hielt, in der alles auf Auflösung zu deuten schien. Und das hat sich in den folgenden Jahren nicht grundsätzlich geändert, obgleich es natürlich den einen oder anderen Abgang gegeben hat, die, um die es einem am meisten leid tut, betrafen die exquisite und elegante Judith Reyn und der Wechsel der temperament-vollen und quecksilbrigen Joyce Cuoco nach München. Von allen deutschen Kompanien hatte Stuttgart während dieser Jahre der Prüfung die geringste Tänzerfluktuation. Es ist in der Tat erstaunlich, und es beweist, daß Cranko etwas in seinen Tänzern gesät hatte, was schwer bei Namen

zu nennen ist, und was jedenfalls mehr als bloße Loyalität sein muß (die sich unvermeidlich über die Jahre abnutzt). Ich selbst bin überzeugt davon, dass es etwas gewesen sein muß, was der Liebe sehr nahekommt.

Als die Kompanie dann diese strenge Prüfungszeit überlebt hatte, die auf seinen Tod folgte, wie groß muss da nicht ihr Erstaunen gewesen sein, als klar wurde, daß, während die Ernennung Glen Tetleys als Crankos Nachfolger ein Zurück zur Normalität zu signalisieren schien, den Anbruch einer neuen Ära, was tatsächlich begonnen hatte, nichts anderes als ihr zweiter Prüfungsab-schnitt war.

Damals schien Tetleys Berufung zwar ein bißchen gewagt, aber doch auch logisch. Tetley war einer der fruchtbarsten Choreographen der Welt, der zwar von der Fakultät des modernen Tanzes kam, aber in jüngster Zeit mehr und mehr Elemente der danse d'école assimiliert hatte. Er hatte durchaus gewinnbringend mit der Kom-panie zusammengearbeitet, und Cranko hatte ihn einge-laden, ständiger Choreograph des Stuttgarter Balletts zu werden. Man kann sich vorstellen, wie perfekt sie einander als Choreographen ergänzt hätten—Cranko als kom-munikativer Dramatiker gegenüber dem reinen und kühlen Formalisten Tetley.

Doch ohne Crankos Anwesenheit entwickelten sich die Dinge ein bißchen zu rein und zu kühl und zu formalistisch für den Geschmack der Tänzer wie auch des Publikums, gar nicht zu reden von den Kritikern. Und der nahezu totale Verzicht auf die Klassiker und Tetleys offenkundiges Desinteresse an der Pflege des Cranko-Repertoires waren auch nicht gerade dazu angetan, das Vertrauen in sein direktoriales Planungskonzept zu stärken, so sehr man ihn auch wegen seiner choreographischen Spezialbegabung geschätzt haben mag (die freilich in vollkommenem Gegensatz zu Crankos Allround-Talent steht).

Man kann sich gut ausmalen, wie frustriert die Tänzer gewesen sein müssen, die bei Cranko aufgewachsen und dazu erzogen worden waren, sich mit ihren Rollen zu identifizieren, und die jetzt mit Tetleys Choreographien konfrontiert waren, in denen von ihnen verlangt wurde, nichts anderes zu projizieren als die Chiffren seiner magistralen Mandarinprosa. Und das um so mehr, wenn sie beobachteten, wie ihnen zur Seite eine ganz andere Art von Tänzern heranwuchs, einige von ihnen noch von Cranko rekrutiert, neben anderen, die von Tetley engagiert worden waren, schnell, schlank, technisch brillant, mit einer sportiven, ja geradezu klinisch abstrakten Vorstellung von Tanz. Man stelle sich einmal vor, was wohl in Haydées Kopf vorgegangen sein muss, einer der bedeutendsten dramatischen Tänzerinnen der Welt, als sie sich schließlich eingestehen mußte, daß Drama passé und funktionelle Bewegungsmechanismen das Gebot der Stunde waren!

Gleichwohl war offenkundig, daß die Kompanie besser

als je zuvor tanzte, und daß da eine Gruppe glänzend begabter Nachwuchstänzer war, die sich ständig verbesserten: Lucia Isenring, Jean Allenby, Melinda Witham, Barry Ingham, Carl Morrow, Mark A. Neal, Christopher Boatwright, Christian Fallanga, um nur die spektakulärsten Kandidaten für künftige Solistenpositionen zu nennen.

Weit weniger offenkundig war, daß auch die Cranko-Tänzer mächtig ausgelegt und eine zusätzliche Elastizität und Biegsamkeit erworben hatten, die ihrem Stil eine neue Dimension erschloß, der einen neuen Glanz und eine neue Politur bekam, ohne auch nur im mindesten etwas von seiner ursprünglichen Gefühlstiefe oder Farbe preiszugeben. Man wurde sich dessen zuerst in den paar Klassikervorstellungen bewußt, die noch übriggeblieben waren—man wurde dessen in den aufregend getanzten Vorstellungen solcher Repertoirejuwelen wie Crankos Initialen R.B.M.E. und MacMillans Lied von der Erde gewahr—und man sah es blühen in dem prächtigen Fortschritt von Birgit Keil, die unter Cranko immer den Eindruck vermittelt hatte, als ob sie kurz vor ihrem grossen Durchbruch stand, der dann doch nie kam, und die unter Tetley endlich ihre Kompetenz als erste Solistin hinter sich liess und ihren rechtmässigen Status als führende klassische Ballerina der Kompanie einnahm, mit Vladimir Klos als ihrem legitimen Danseur-noble-Gemahl.

Was indessen leicht hätte passieren können, war, daß Haydée und Cragun und Madsen, unzufrieden mit dem Tetley-Regime, die Kompanie verlassen hätten, um als freischaffende Tänzer Karriere zu machen (Clauss war dazu ausersehen, die Nachfolge von Anne Woolliams als Direktor der John-Cranko-Schule anzutreten), während nahezu jede Kompanie in Deutschland und viele im Ausland mit Kußhand Keil als Primaballerina engagiert hätten—eine Stellung, die Stuttgart ihr verweigerte—, mit Klos als Partner. Doch genau das trat eben nicht ein! Das Stuttgarter Ballett bestand seine zweite, die Tetley-Probe mit Auszeichnung. Die ursprüngliche Cranko-Equipe blieb da und vermischte sich auf liebenswerteste Weise und ganz harmonisch mit den Tetley-Novizen. Und als Tetley dann zum Ende der Spielzeit 1975/76 zurücktrat, offenbar endgültig davon überzeugt, dass er keine Chance hatte, vom Stuttgarter Publikum und der Kritik je akzeptiert zu werden, gab es zumindest vereinzelte Versuche, seinen Leistungen objektiv gerecht zu werden. Wenigstens diejenigen, die bereit waren, den Dingen unvoreingenommen ins Gesicht zu sehen, mußten zugeben, daß die Kompanie vorher nie besser ausgesehen und getanzt hatte, und daß Tetley dem Repertoire zumindest ein paar Ballette beigesteuert hatte, die jede Kompanie der Welt stolz wäre, zu besitzen, um nur Voluntaries, Laborintus, Pierrot Lunaire und Le Sacre du printemps zu nennen.

Daß das Stuttgarter Ballett diese schwierigen Jahre nach Crankos Tod überlebte, war, was ich Stuttgarts zweites Ballettwunder nenne. Mit der Übernahme der Künstlerischen Direktion durch Haydée zur Spielzeit 1976/77—eine Entscheidung, die nach vielerlei Beratungen zwischen den Generalintendanten Hans-Peter Doll und dem Tänzern gefällt wurde—schien sich endgültig eine Rückkehr zu normalen Verhältnissen anzubahnen.

Das bedeutete natürlich nicht, daß die Tetley-Episode völliger Vergessenheit anheimgefallen wäre, oder daß versucht worden wäre, da anzuknüpfen, wo Cranko hatte aufgeben müssen. Das konnte schon deswegen nicht der Fall sein, weil Haydée keine Choreographin ist und deshalb ständig Ausschau nach Choreographen halten muss, die nicht nur bereit sind, ihre schon vorhandenen Ballette einzustudieren, sondern neue Werke speziell für die Kompanie zu choreographieren—was ein sehr schwieriger Job ist, bedenkt man, daß heutzutage alle Spitzenchoreographen fest der einen oder anderen Kompanie liiert sind.

In ihrer ersten Spielzeit, war Haydée, die ja auch weiterhin tanzt, und die man deswegen nicht gut mit anderen weltberühmten Ballettdirektorinnen wie Marie Rambert, Ninette de Valois, Lucia Chase oder Beryl Grey vergleichen kann, überaus erfolgreich. Einmal indem es ihr gelang, MacMillan erneut nach Stuttgart zu locken, wo er sein ungemein anrührendes Requiem zu Faurés Musik choreographierte, das nicht wenige für sein bisher bestes Ballett überhaupt halten. Und zum zweiten, indem sie mit Rosella Hightowers Einstudierung von Dornröschen nicht nur die lange überfällige Rückkehr zu einer Politik bekräftigte, die die Klassiker für eine Kompanie, wie sie das Stuttgarter Ballett darstellt, als Fundament begreift, sondern indem sie auch die Publikumsbegeisterung erneuerte, die in den letzten Jahren ein bißchen schlaff geworden war.

Mit der Ankündigung neuer Ballette von John Neumeier und Jiri Kylián und der Fortsetzung der Zusammenarbeit mit MacMillan für die Spielzeit 1977/78 scheint sie fest entschlossen, den Leitlinien zu folgen, die Cranko vorgezeichnet hatte, und die in eine genuin kreative Zukunft weisen. Besser noch: in ihrer ersten Spielzeit, ist es Haydée, deren faszinierende Ausstrahlung als Tanz-Aktrice in keiner Weise nachgelassen hat, gelungen, nach Kräften ein paar höchst bemerkenswerte Tänzernachwuchstalente zu fördern, darunter Eileen Brady, Sylviane Bayard, Nora Kimball, Kurt Speker und Stephen Greenston. Darüber hinaus hat sie dafür gesorgt, daß ein paar andere Tänzer wie Reid Anderson und Marcis Lesins neue, sie herausfordernde Rollen bekommen haben und ihnen dadurch geholfen, ihre Kunst weiter zu kultivieren. Und in William Forsythe hat sie unter den Corps-Tänzern ein vehement sich ankündigendes choreographisches Temperament entdeckt, das sich, wie man hoffen darf, in der Linie der Neumeier und Kylián entfalten wird (ohne daß auch er notwendigerweise die Kompanie verlässt).

So scheint denn das Stuttgarter Ballett zu Beginn der

Spielzett 1977/78, der siebzehnten Spielzeit nach der Ernennung Crankos als Ballettdirektor, unmittelbar nach seiner fünften amerikanischen Tournee, die schlimmsten Prüfungen seiner jungen Geschichte hinter sich zu haben und dabei zu sein, in seinen zweiten Entwicklungsabschnitt einzutreten, von dem jeder, der der Kompanie wohlgesonnen ist, hofft, daß er eine Ära unbegrenzter Kreativität sein wird.

Auf jeden Fall steht der alte Cranko-Geist des Zusammengehörigkeitsgefühls wieder in voller Blüte, und man registriert beglückt erneut jene starke Glücksausstrahlung, durch die sich das Stuttgarter Ballett von den meisten westlichen Ballettkompanien unterscheidet (darin scheinen sie die Vettern ersten Grades der Königlichen Dänen zu sein). Möge es ihnen noch lange vergönnt sein, ihre Freudenbotschaft zu verbreiten! Unsere Welt der späten siebziger Jahre ist ihrer dringend bedürftig!

Marcia Haydée, Richard Cragun

Romeo and Juliet

Romeo und Julia

1. Egon Madsen (Romeo)   2. Ball scene   3. Marcia Haydée, Richard Cragun

1. Egon Madsen (Mercutio)
2. Barry Ingham, Christian Fallanga, Eileen Brady
3. Marcia Haydée
4. Marcia Haydée, Richard Cragun

1. Joyce Cuoco, Egon Madsen
2. Eileen Brady, Barry Ingham
3. Marcia Haydée, Richard Cragun
4. Eileen Brady, Barry Ingham
5. Marcia Haydée, Richard Cragun

4

5

1. Dale Brannon, Melissa Lyons, Mark A. Neal, Jacqui Gorden, Peter Connell   2. Act 2   3. Richard Cragun (Romeo)

1. Egon Madsen (Romeo)
2. Richard Cragun (Mercutio), Carl Morrow
3. Egon Madsen, Ulf Esser, Lucia Montagnon
4. Jan Stripling, Egon Madsen (Mercutio)

Mercutio's death /
Mercutios Tod
1. Barry Ingham
(Mercutio)
2. Egon Madsen
(Mercutio)
3. Carl Morrow, Egon
Madsen, Richard Cragun

3

2

1. Egon Madsen, Marcis Lesins
2. Ruth Papendick, Jan Stripling
3. Joyce Cuoco, Egon Madsen
4. Birgit Keil, Vladimir Klos

3

4

1. Eileen Brady, Ulf Esser
2. Marcis Lesins, Marcia
Haydée
3. Kurt Speker
4 & 5. Marcia Haydée,
Richard Cragun

Opus 1

2

3

1, 2 & 3. Birgit Keil,
Richard Cragun

1–18. Egon Madsen making up for the Joker in *Jeu de cartes*

1–18. *Egon Madsen beim Schminken für* Jeu de cartes

Jeu de cartes

1. Egon Madsen
2. Dale Brannon, Teresina Mosco, Christian Fallanga
3. Angela Schmidt, Egon Madsen
4. Birgit Keil, Mark A. Neal

1. Mark A. Neal (Joker)
2. Carl Morrow, Stephen Greenston,
Christopher Boatwright, Michael Wasmund,
William Forsythe
3. Christopher Boatwright
4. William Forsythe
5. Egon Madsen

3

4

5

Onegin

1. Marcia Haydée
2. Marcia Haydée, Richard Cragun
3. Eileen Brady, Egon Madsen

3

1. Act 1
2. Eileen Brady, Michael Wasmund
3. Marcia Haydée, Richard Cragun
4. Eileen Brady, Michael Wasmund
5. Marcia Haydée, Richard Cragun

5

1 & 3. Marcia Haydée, Richard Cragun
2. Marcia Haydée

4. Michael Wasmund, Richard Cragun
5. Birgit Keil, Vladimir Klos

1 & 2. Marcia Haydée, Reid Anderson
3. Barry Ingham
4. Marcia Haydée, Richard Cragun
5 & 6. Birgit Keil, Vladimir Klos

4

5

6

Initials R.B.M.E.

Initialen R.B.M.E.

1 & 2. Richard Cragun
3. Birgit Keil
4. Melinda Witham,
Christopher Boatwright

1 & 2. Marcia Haydée, Heinz Clauss   3. Marcia Haydée, Birgit Keil, Richard Cragun, Egon Madsen   4. Jean Allenby,
Reid Anderson

1

4

5

6

1. Sylviane Bayard   2. Egon Madsen   3. Birgit Keil, Jean Allenby, Richard Cragun, Egon Madsen   4. Christopher Boatwright   5. Egon Madsen, Otto Neubert   6. Class / *Training*

Greening

Poème de l'extase

3

4

1. Greening
2. Nora Kimball, Christopher Boatwright
3. Marcia Haydée, Egon Madsen
4. Reid Anderson, Marcia Haydée, Egon Madsen

Der Widerspenstigen Zähmung
The Taming of the Shrew

1. Marcia Haydée, Richard Cragun
2. Vladimir Klos
3. Richard Cragun

1. Sylviane Bayard, Barry Ingham
2 & 3. Marcia Haydée, Richard
Cragun

3

1

2

3

1–4. Marcia Haydée, Richard Cragun

1. Marcia Haydée, Richard Cragun
2. Richard Cragun, Marcia Haydée,
Douglas Horacek
3. Richard Cragun

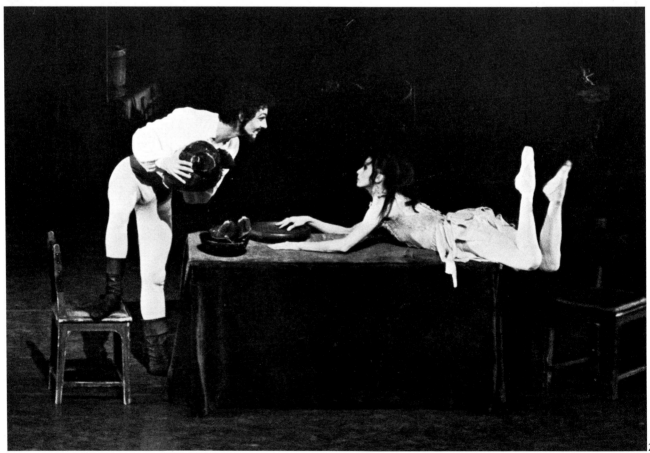

2

3

4

1 & 2. Birgit Keil, Vladimir Klos
3 & 4. Marcia Haydée
5. Marcia Haydée, Richard
Cragun

1. Sylviane Bayard, Kurt Speker
2. Birgit Keil, Vladimir Klos
3. Lucia Montagnon, Reid Anderson
4. Sylviane Bayard, Kurt Speker

1. Marcia Haydée, Richard Cragun   2. Birgit Keil, Vladimir Klos   3. Eileen Brady, Barry Ingham

Voluntaries

1

2

4

3

5

1, 2, 3 & 4. Marcia Haydée, Richard Cragun
5. Eileen Brady, Barry Ingham
6, 7 & 8. Birgit Keil, Vladimir Klos, Reid Anderson

7

1. Birgit Keil, Vladimir Klos,
Reid Anderson
2. Marcia Haydée, Richard
Cragun
3 & 4. *Corps de ballet*

3

4

The Sleeping Beauty
Dornröschen

1 & 2. Marcia Haydée   3. Hilde Koch   4. Birgit Keil, Reid Anderson

1. Birgit Keil   2. Richard Cragun
3 & 4. Birgit Keil

2

1. Jean Allenby, Vladimir Klos
2. Birgit Keil, Vladimir Klos
3. Lucia Montagnon
(Bluebird / *Blauer pas de deux*)

1. Eileen Brady, Egon Madsen
Bluebird / *Blauer pas de deux*:
2. Eileen Brady, Carl Morrow
3. Lucia Montagnon, Richard
Cragun
4. Richard Cragun

1. Pierre Wyss, Mark A. Neal, Stephen Greenston   2, 3 & 4. Birgit Keil, Vladimir Klos

Song of the Earth

Das Lied von der Erde

1

2

3

1. Marcia Haydée, Richard
Cragun
2. Marcia Haydée, Richard
Cragun, Egon Madsen
3. Egon Madsen
4. Richard Cragun

4

1. Sarah Abendroth, Ray Barra,
Oranna Hammerle
2. Birgit Keil
3. Megan Hintz, Lucia Montagnon
4. Birgit Keil, Reid Anderson,
Egon Madsen, Richard Cragun

Innere Not   **Inner Need**

1. Reid Anderson, Richard Cragun, Egon Madsen, Vladimir Klos   2. Egon Madsen, Richard Cragun   3. Richard Cragun

Daphne

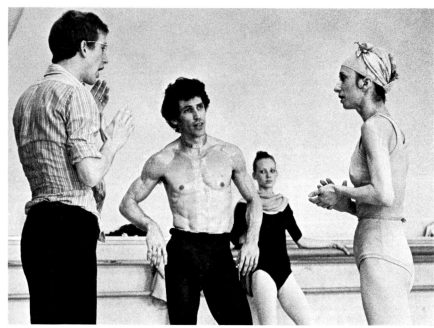

1. Marcia Haydée, Richard Cragun
2. William Forsythe, Richard
Cragun, Marcia Haydée
3. Marcia Haydée, Richard Cragun

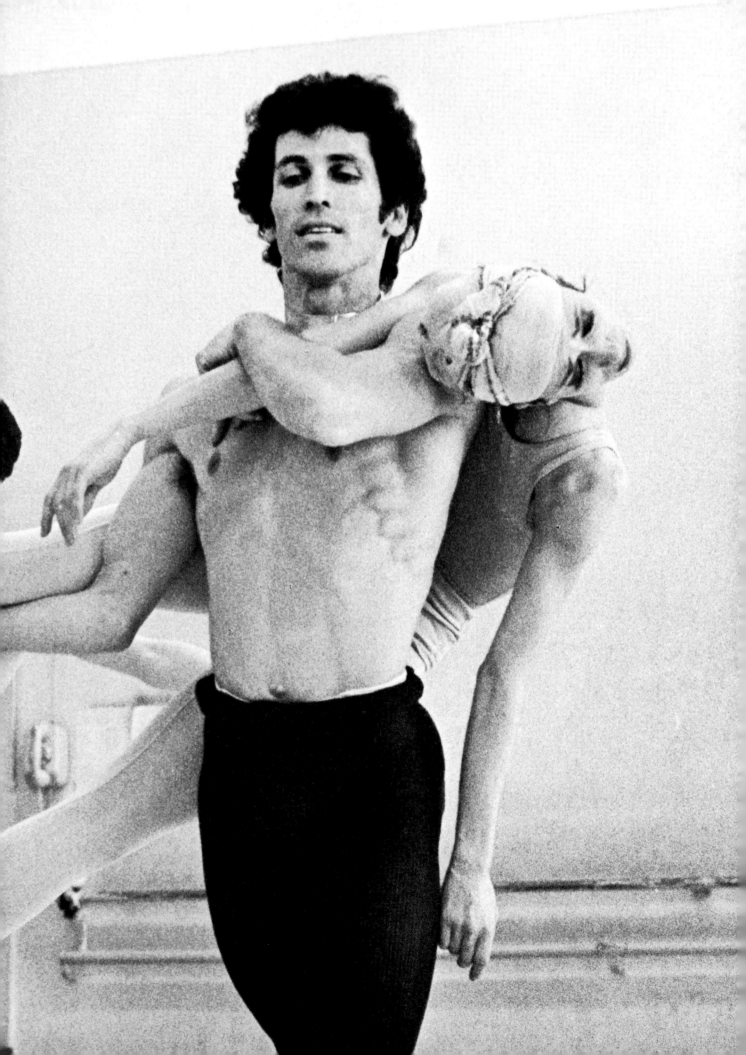

1, 2, 3 & 4. Marcia Haydée,
Richard Cragun

1

2

3

1. Richard Cragun
2 & 3. Marcia Haydée,
Richard Cragun
4. Stephen Greenston
5. Egon Madsen, Johannes
Kritzinger

1

1. Alan Beale
2. Birgit Keil
3. Marcia Haydée, Richard
Cragun

2

Daphnis and Chloë
Daphnis und Chloë

3

1. Richard Cragun, Egon
Madsen
2. *Corps de ballet*
3. Marcia Haydée, Richard
Cragun
4. Egon Madsen, Richard
Cragun

4

1, 2 & 3. Birgit Keil, Richard Cragun
4. (L–R) Lucia Montagnon, Egon Madsen, Richard Cragun, Marcia Haydée

Der Fall Hamlet   Hamlet

1. Egon Madsen, Richard Cragun
2. Egon Madsen, Lucia
Montagnon, Reid Anderson
3. Richard Cragun, Reid
Anderson

3

1

1. Egon Madsen
2. Richard Cragun, Marcia
Haydée, Egon Madsen
3. Marcia Haydée

2

3

1. Lucia Montagnon, Egon
Madsen
2. Reid Anderson, Egon
Madsen, Lucia Montagnon
3. Egon Madsen, Reid
Anderson

La Valse

2

3

1. Egon Madsen, Richard
Cragun, Reid Anderson,
Marcia Haydée
2. Birgit Keil, Vladimir Klos
3. Hilde Koch, Barry
Ingham, Kathryn Bennets

1. Alexander Ursuliak
2. Rosella Hightower
3. Michèle Rabier

Requiem

1. *Pie Jesu:* Marcia Haydée   2. *Introitus:* Birgit Keil, Richard Cragun   3. *Introitus:* Marcia Haydée, *Corps de ballet*

1. *Introitus:* Marcia Haydée, *Corps de ballet*   2. *Corps de ballet*   3. *Offertorium:* Marcia Haydée, Richard Cragun

1, 2 & 3. *Offertorium:*
Marcia Haydée, Richard Cragun

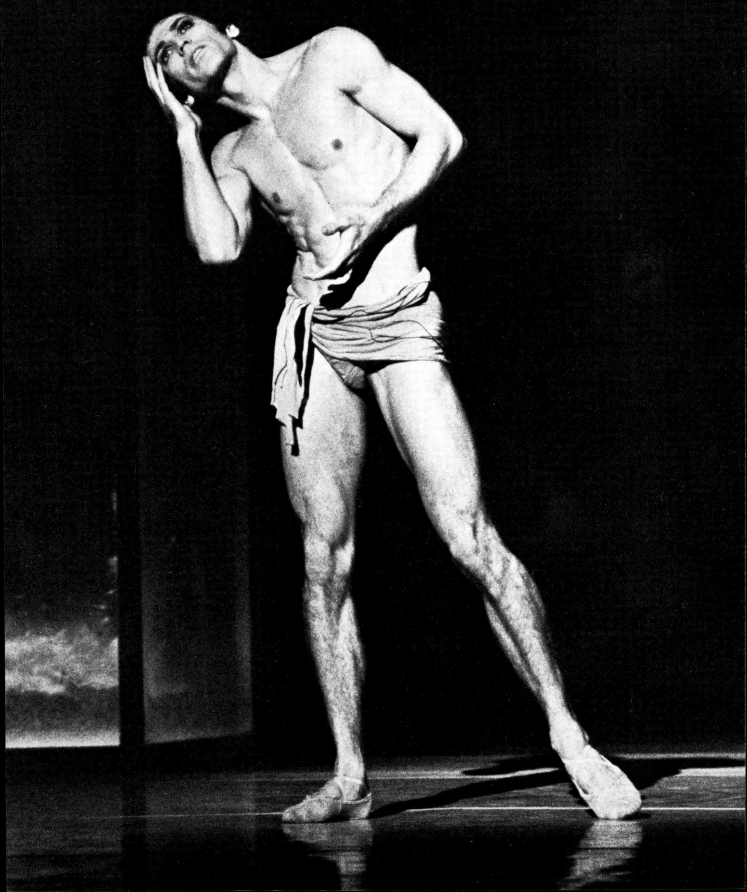

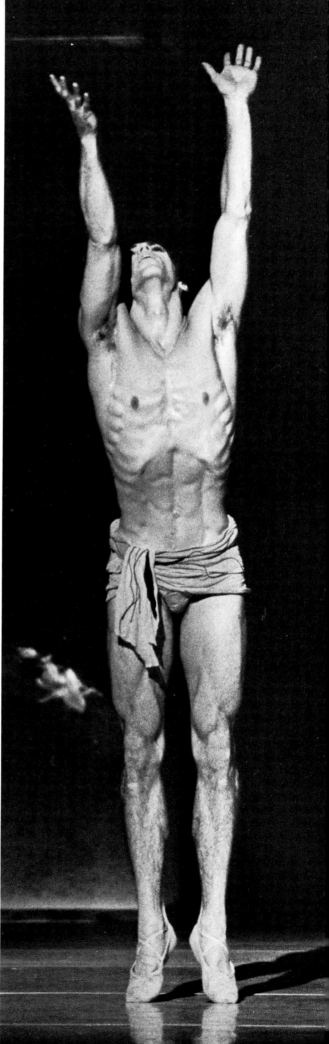

1, 2, 3 & 4. *Offertorium:* Richard Cragun

1. *Offertorium:* Richard Cragun   2. *Sanctus:* Marcia Haydée, Reid Anderson

2

1 & 2. *Sanctus:* Marcia Haydée, Reid Anderson
3. *Pie Jesu:* Marcia Haydée

1. *Pie Jesu:* Marcia Haydée
2 & 3. *Agnus Dei:* Birgit Keil
4. *Agnus Dei:* Birgit Keil, Mark A.
Neal, Simon Dow, Kurt Speker,
Christian Fallanga

2

3

1. *Agnus Dei:* Marcia Haydée, Birgit Keil, Mark A. Neal, Simon Dow, Kurt Speker   2. *Libera me*   3. *Libera me:* Egon Madsen, Barry Ingham, Carl Morrow, Kurt Speker

1. *Libera me:* Egon Madsen,
Barry Ingham
2. *Libera me:* Carl Morrow,
Egon Madsen, Reid Anderson,
Barry Ingham
3. *Libera me:* Reid Anderson,
Egon Madsen

1. *Libera me:* (L–R) Simon Dow, Kurt Speker, Egon Madsen, Mark A. Neal, Christopher Boatwright   2. *In Paradisum:*
(L–R) Barry Ingham, Marcia Haydée, Egon Madsen, Reid Anderson, Richard Cragun, Birgit Keil
(Overleaf / *Auf der nächsten Seite.*) *In Paradisum:* Marcia Haydée, Richard Cragun, Reid Anderson